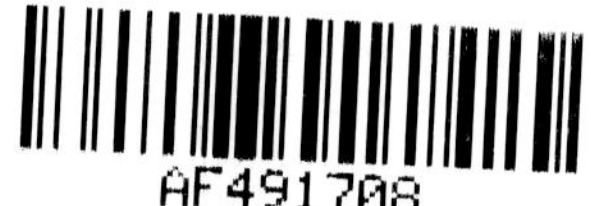

Animal Coloring Book

Lion

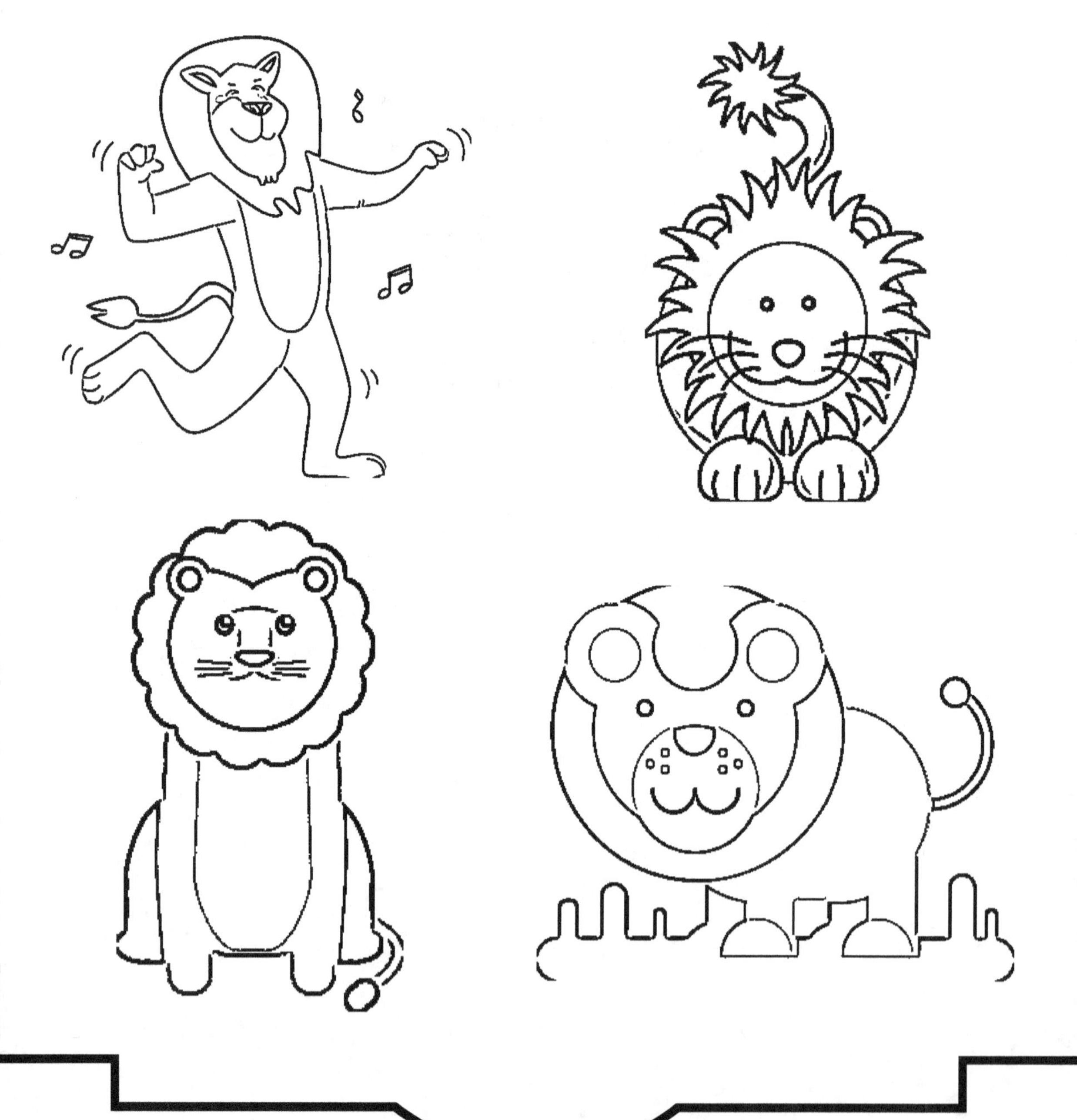

Elephant

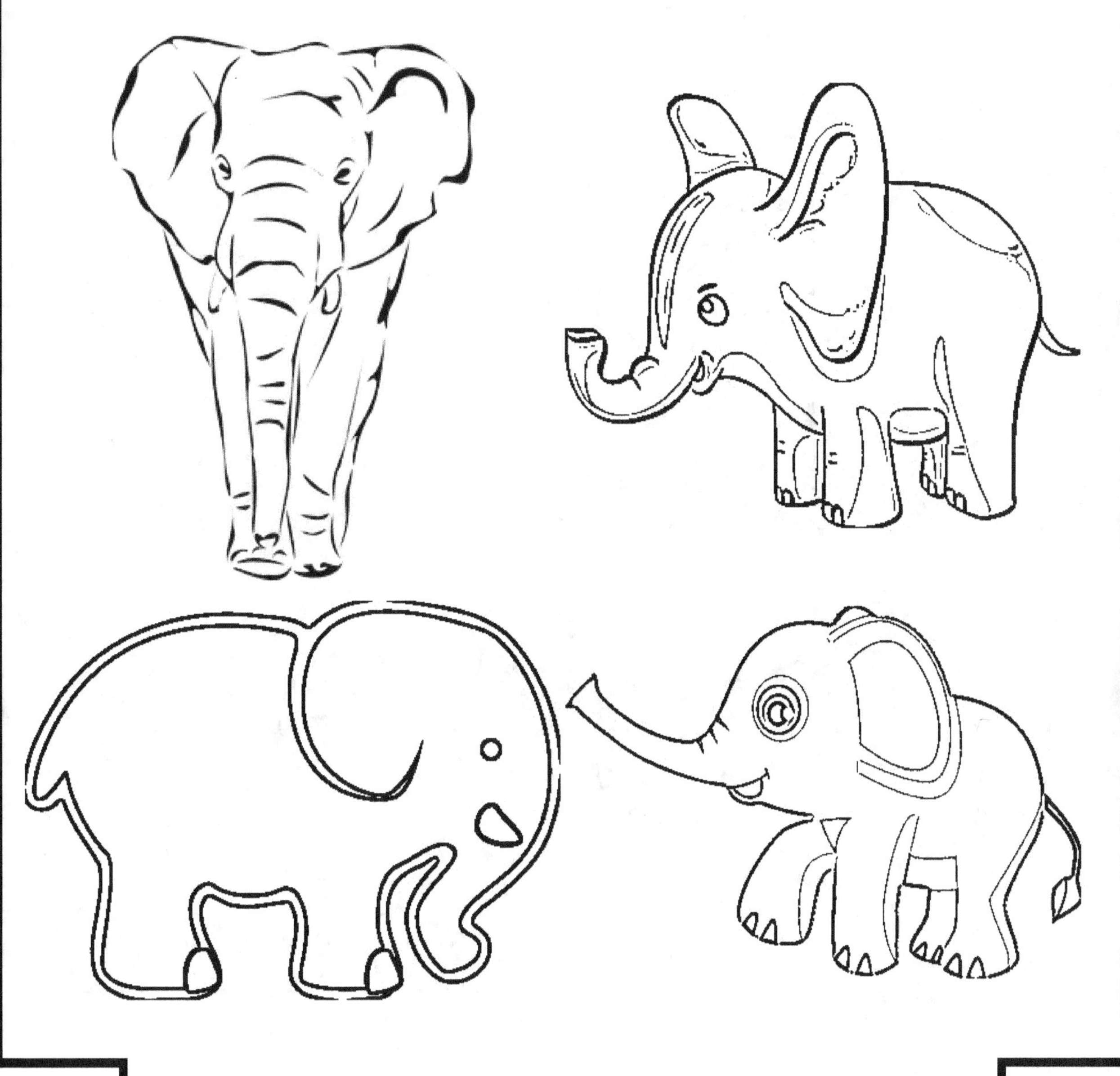

Sheep

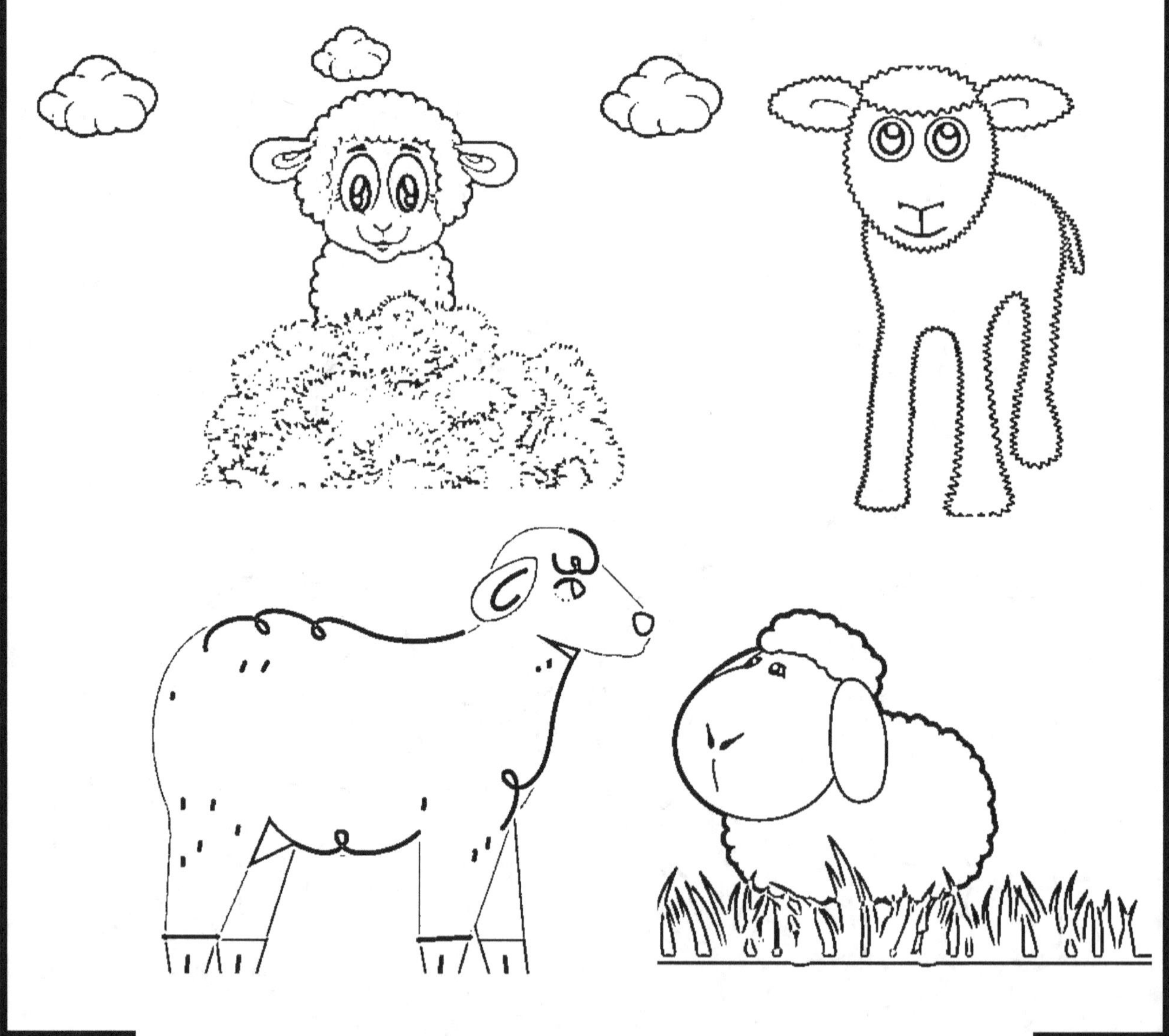

Cow

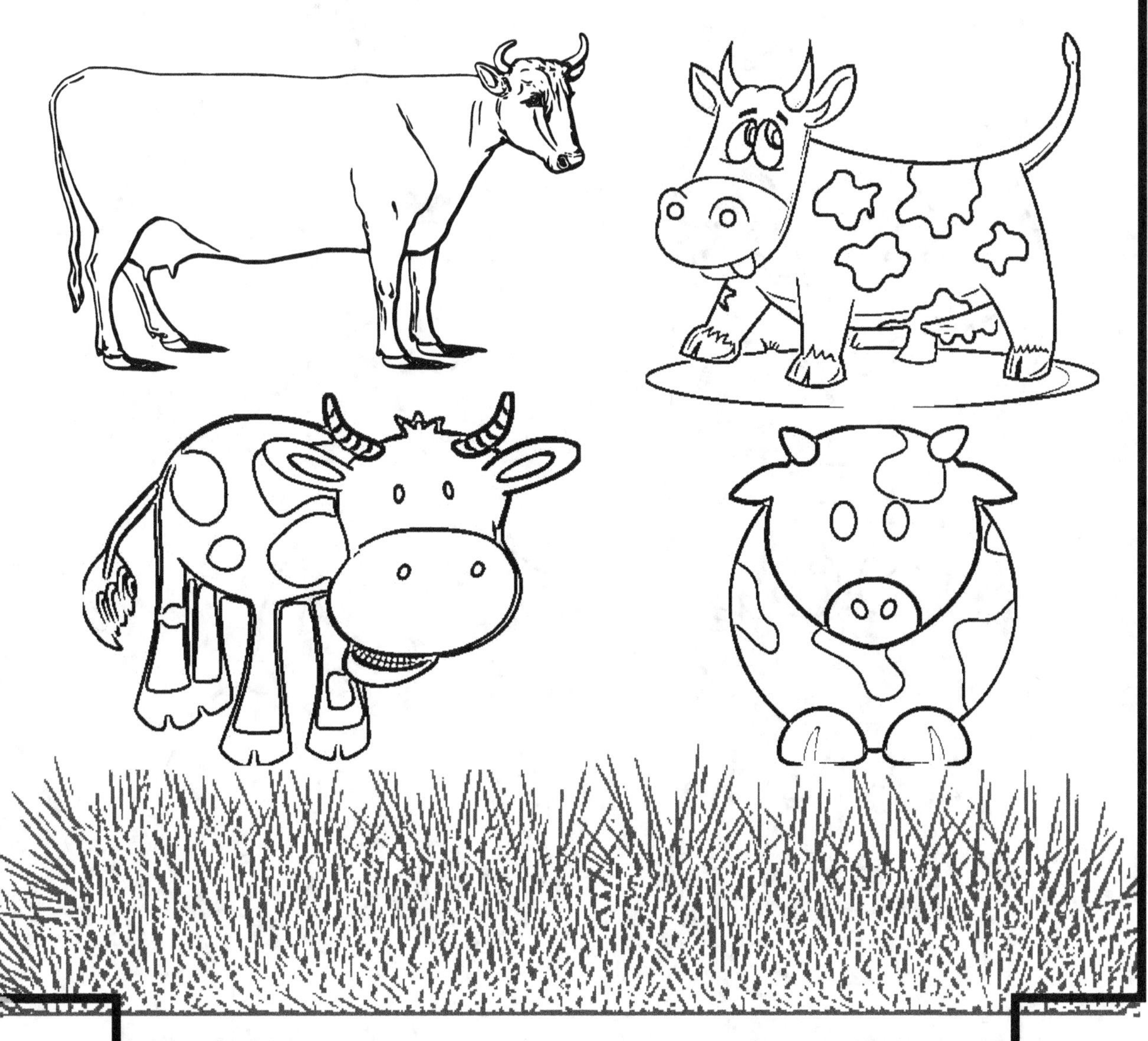

Cat

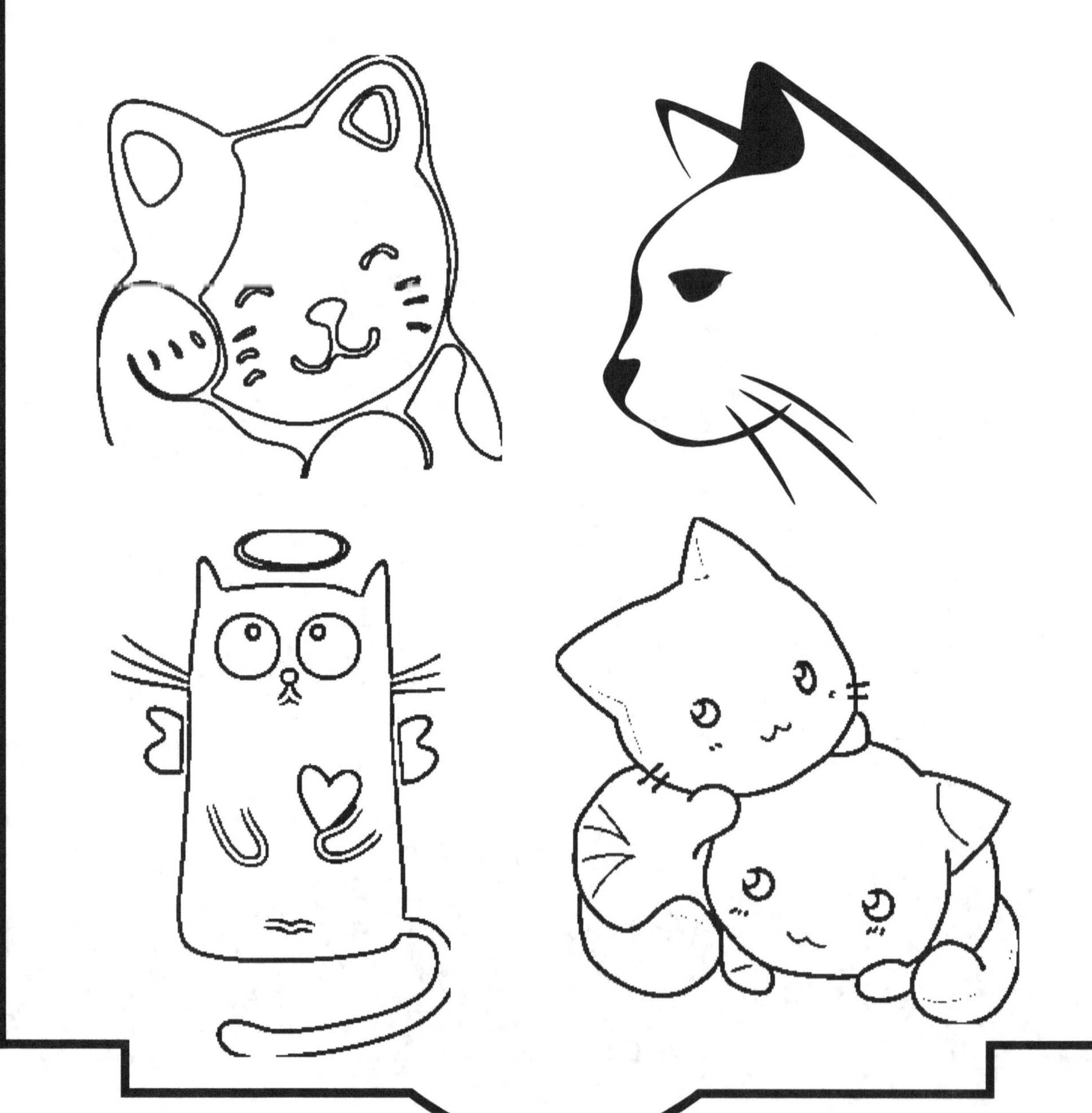

Butterfly

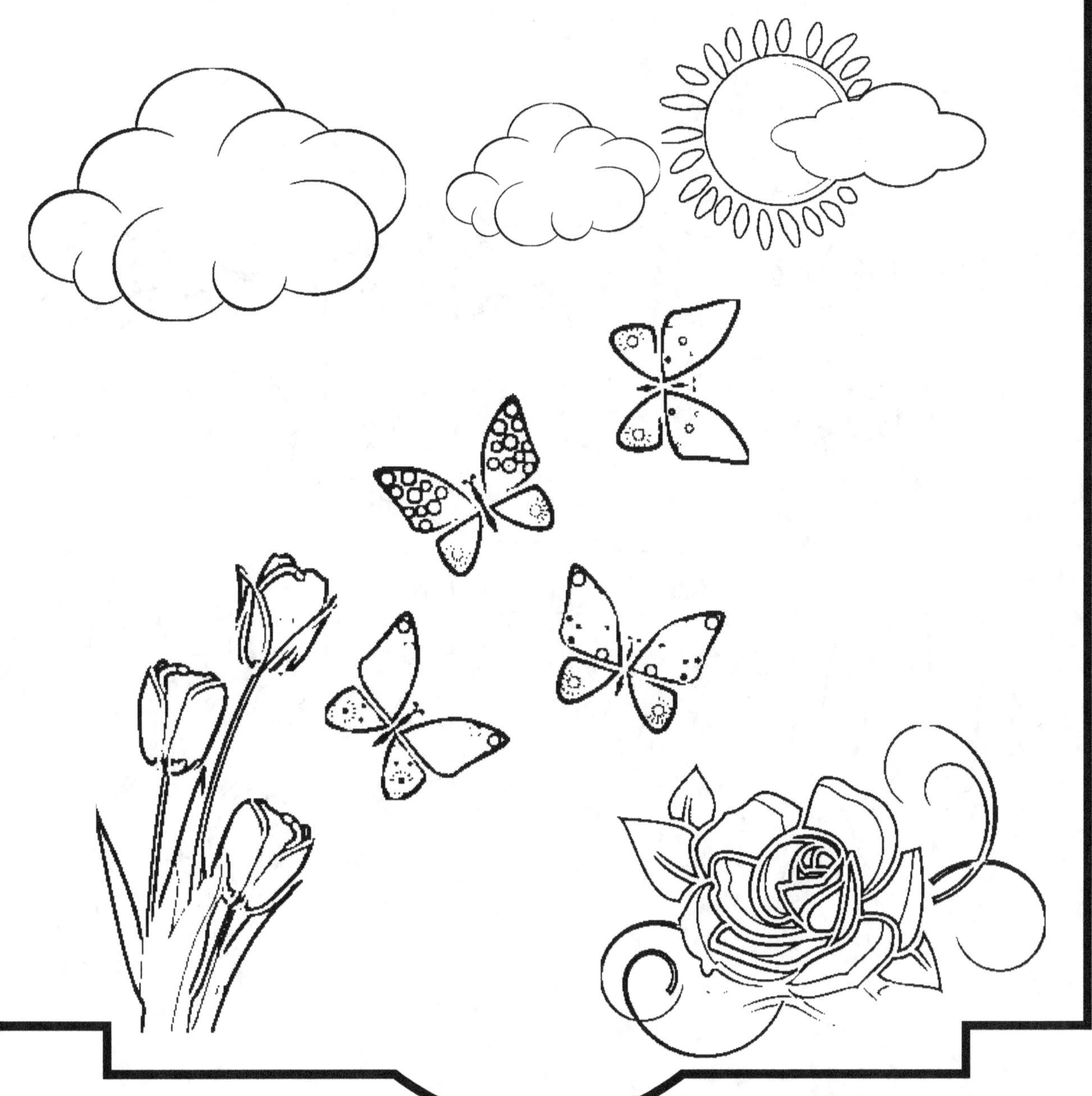

Fish

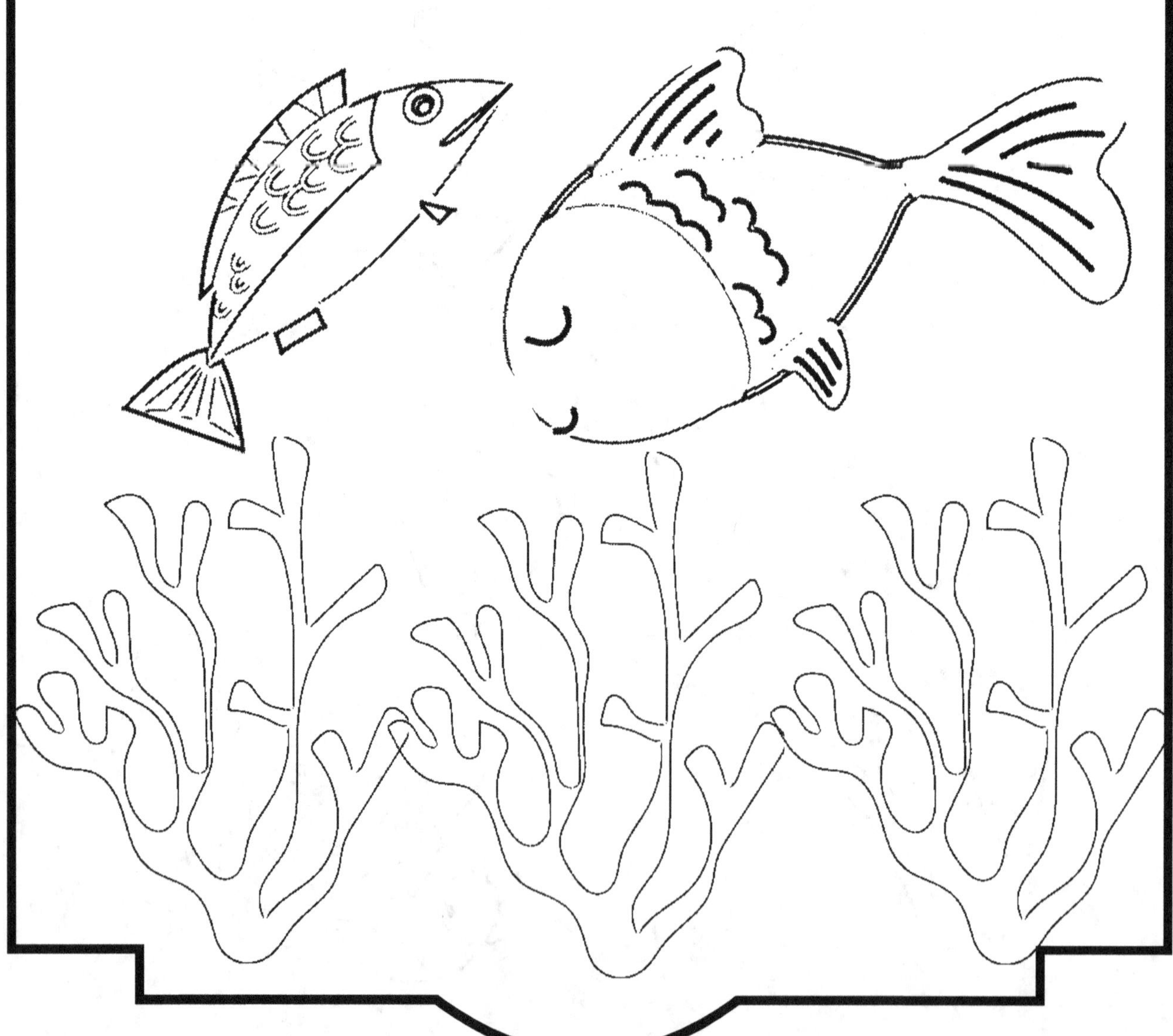

Dog

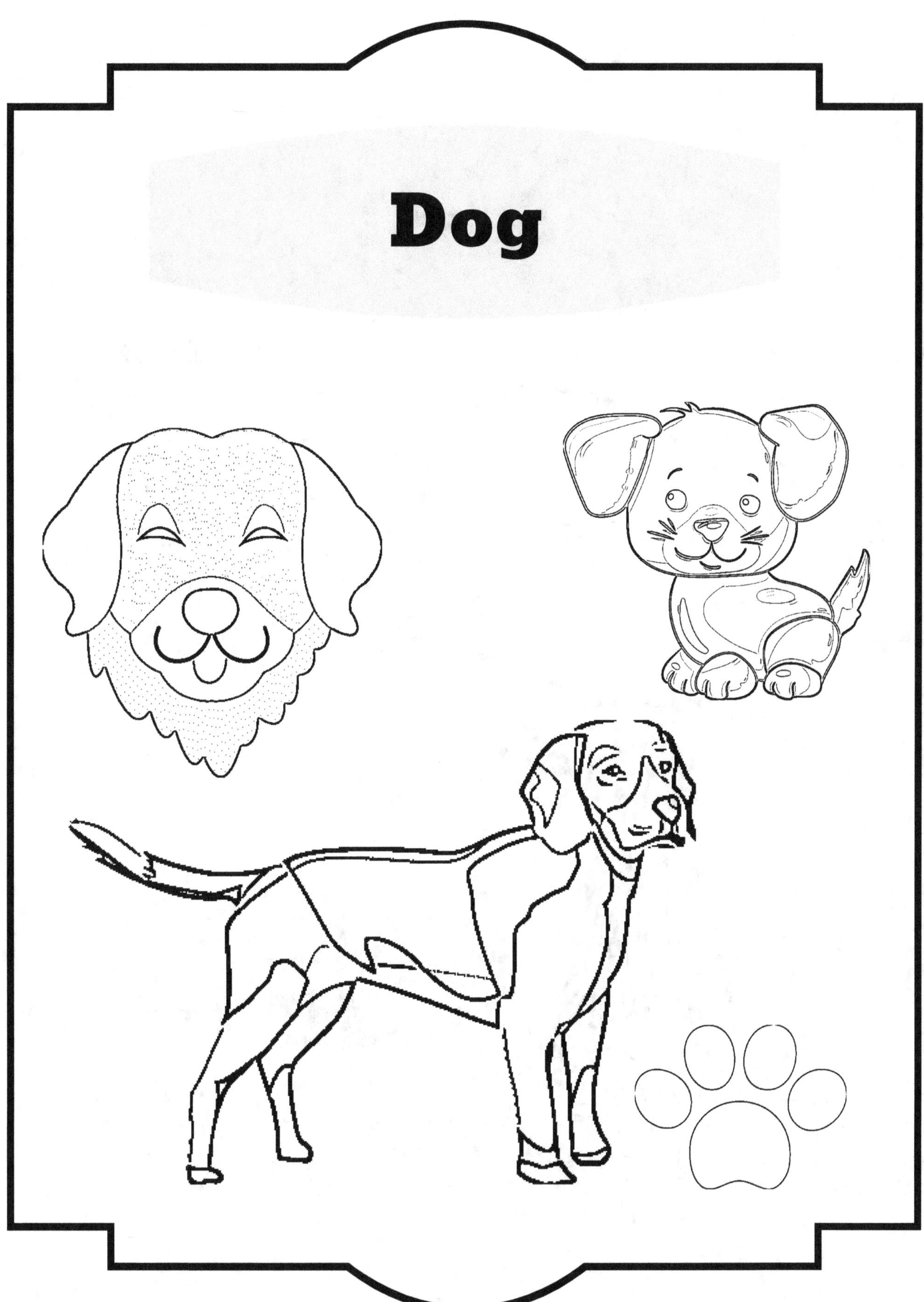

Snail

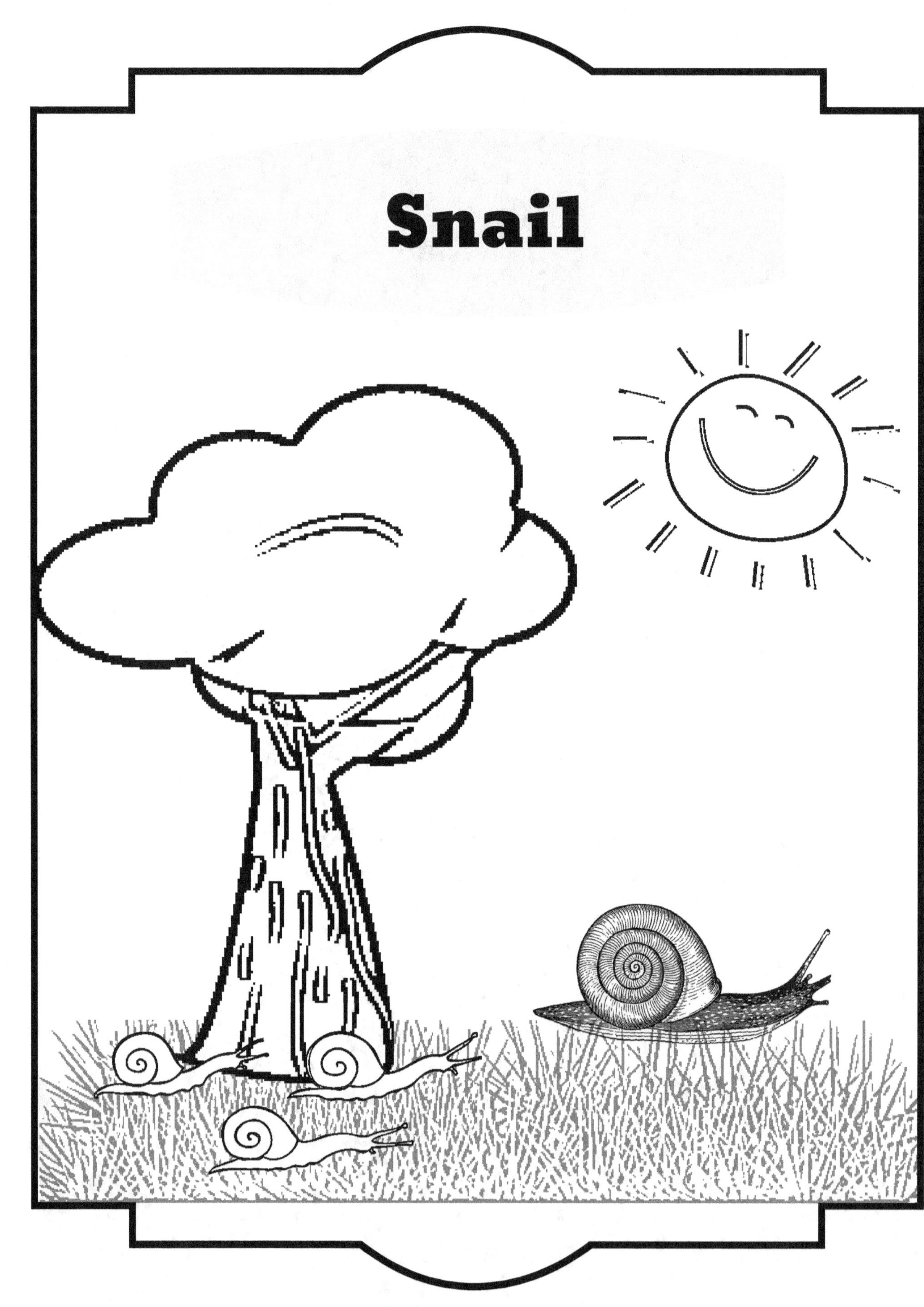

Koala

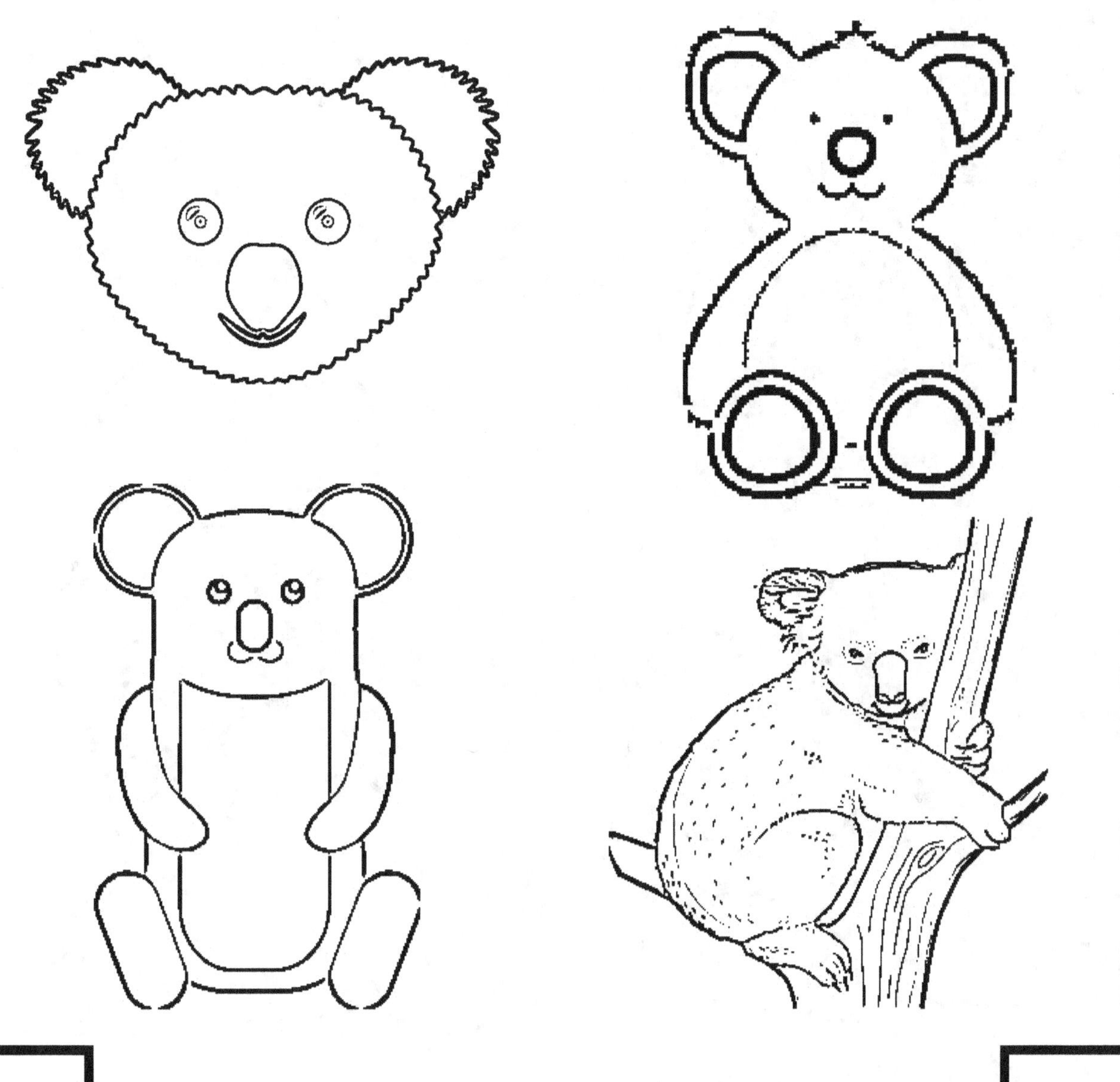

Panda

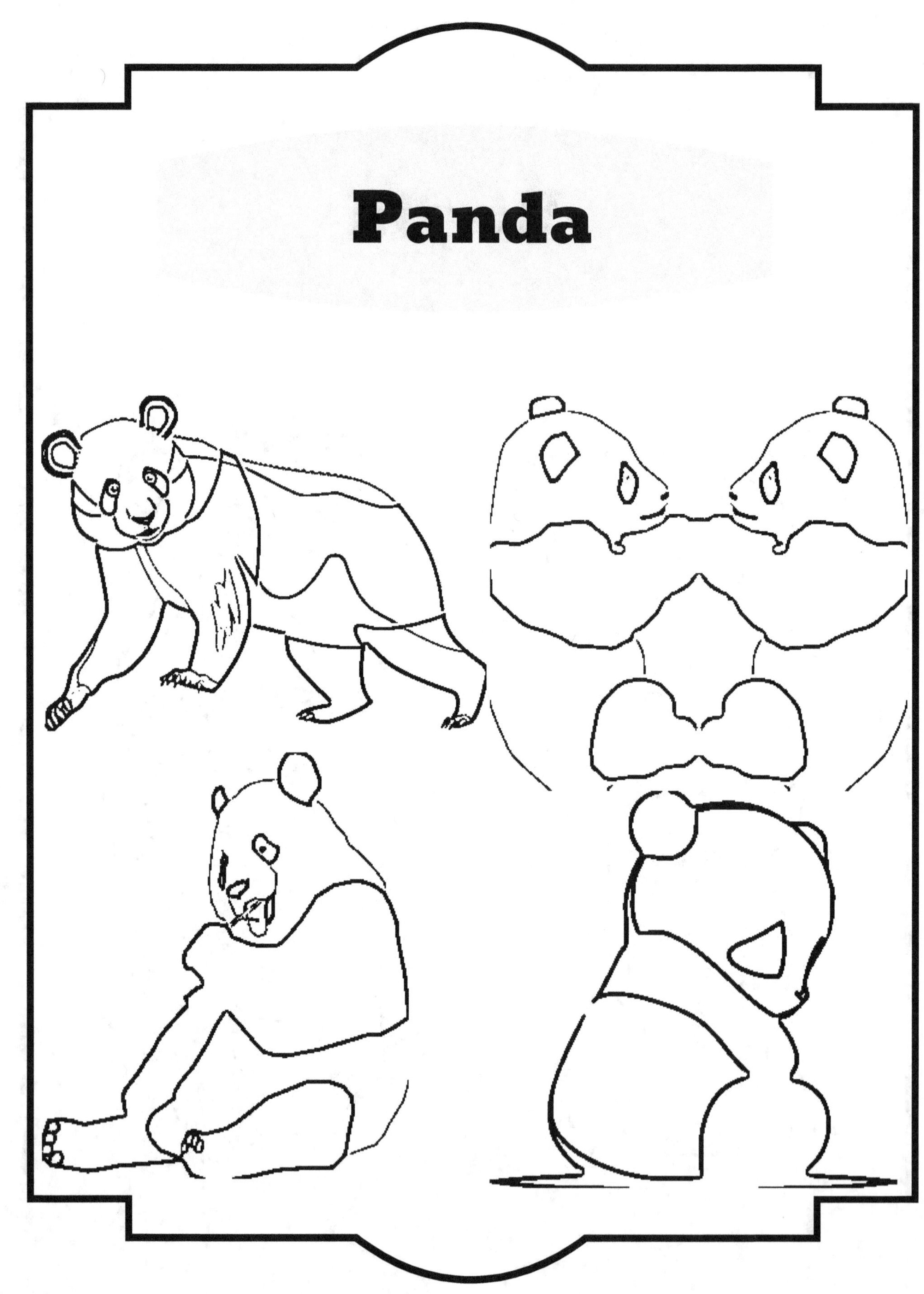

Giraffe

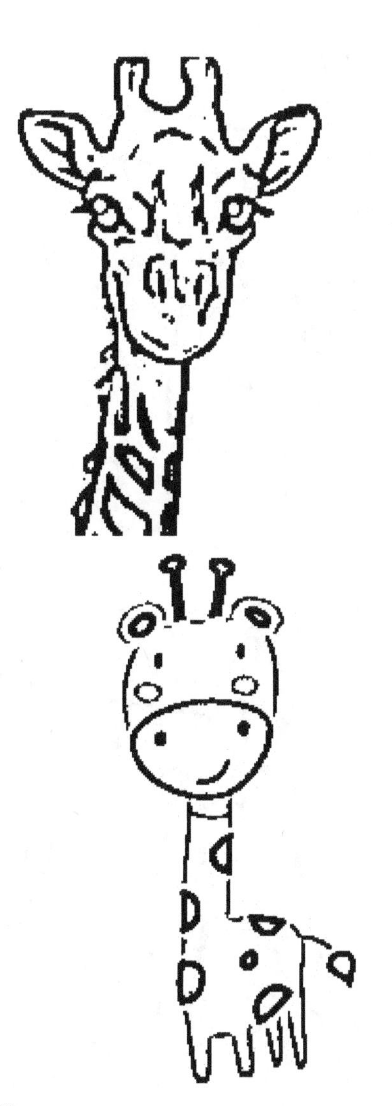 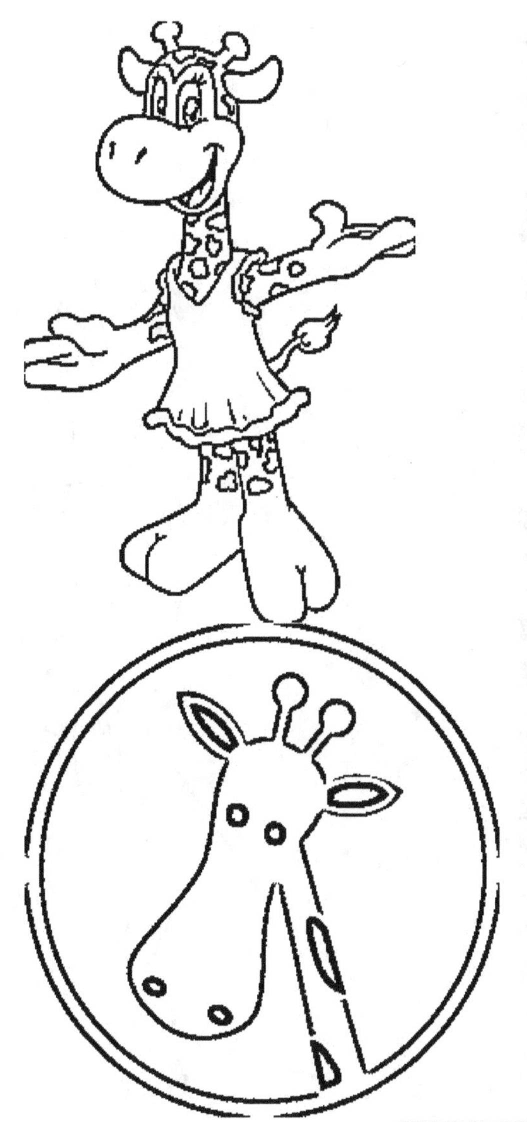

Kangaroo

Horse

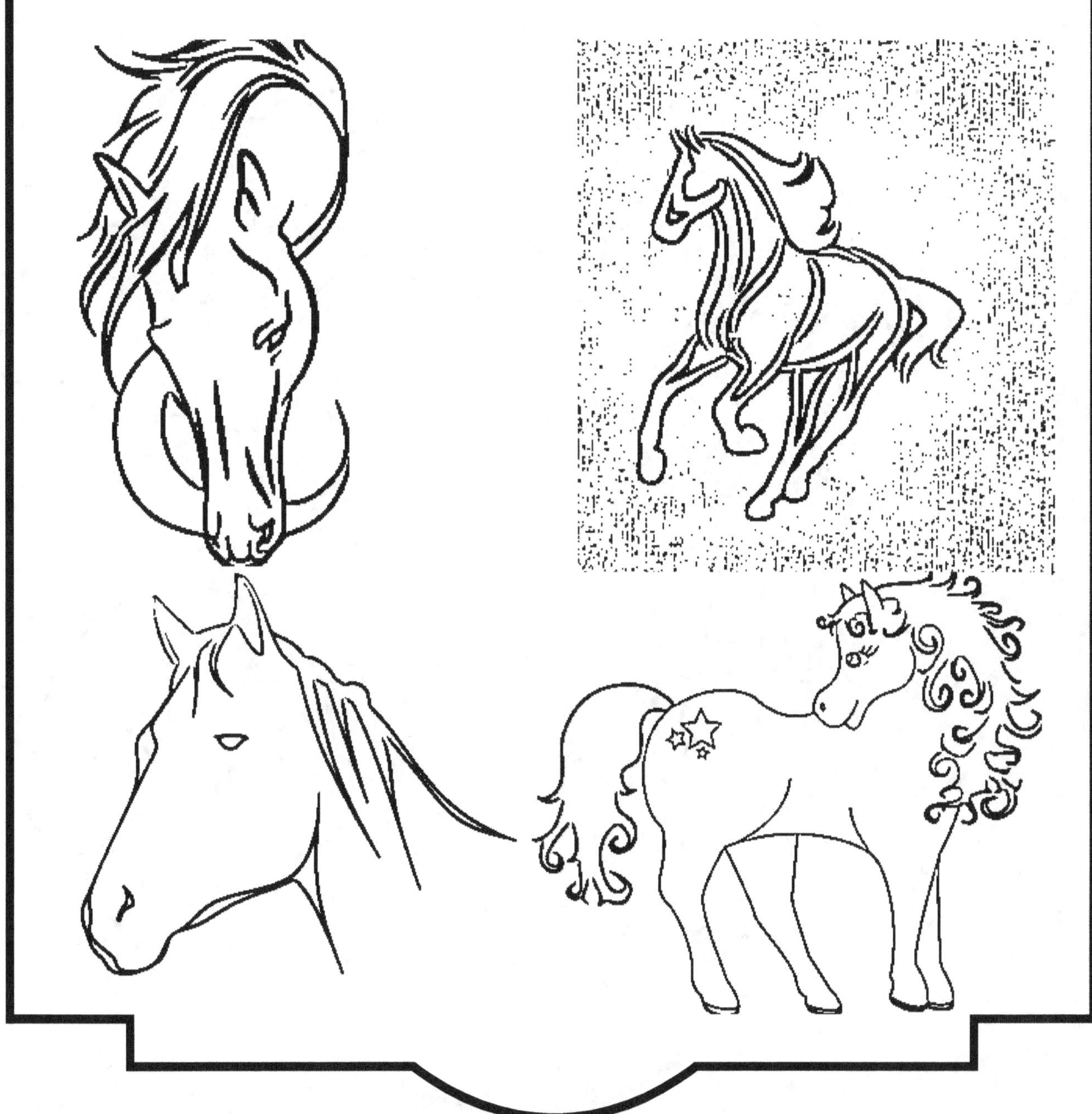

Mouse

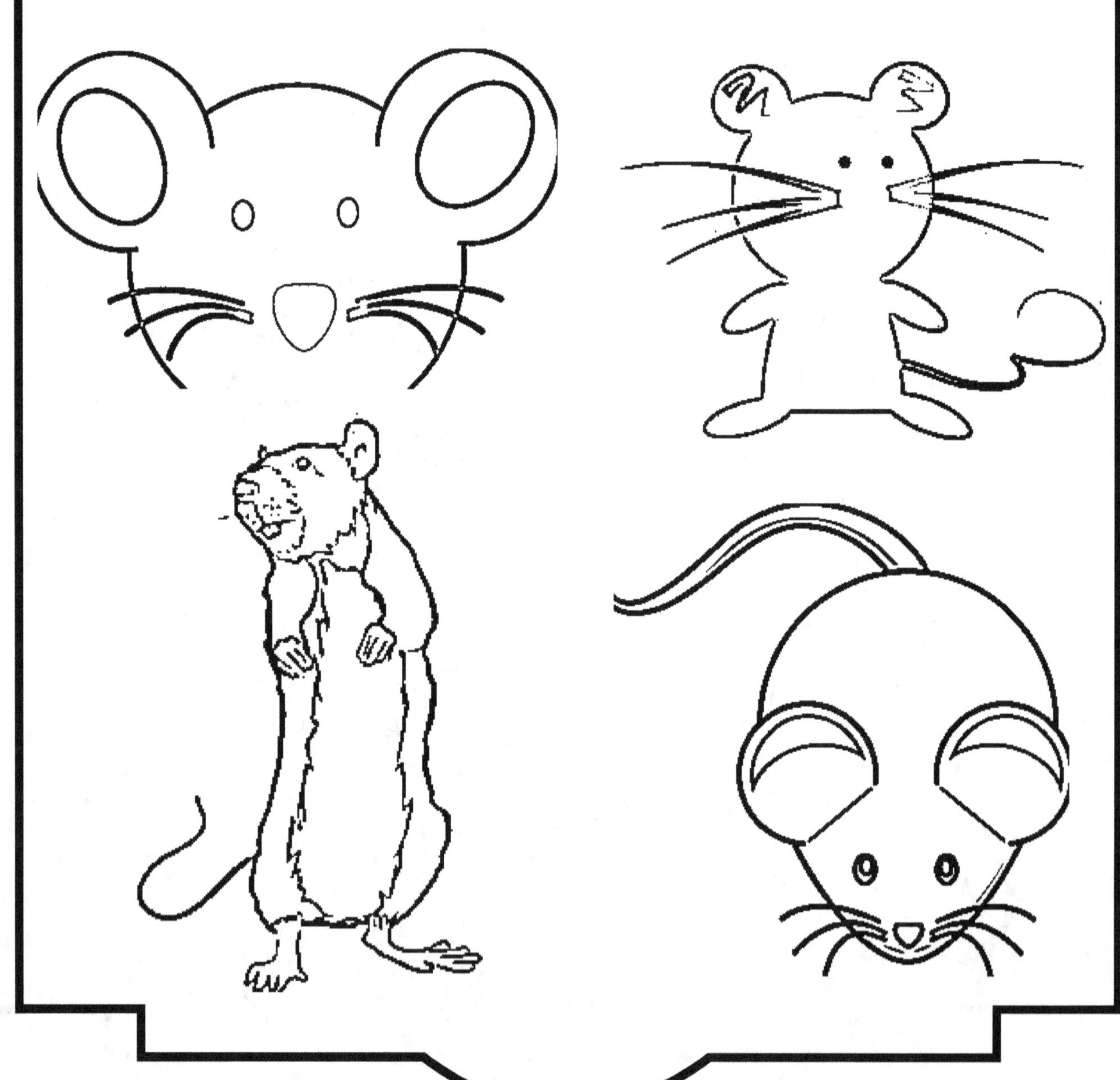

Frog

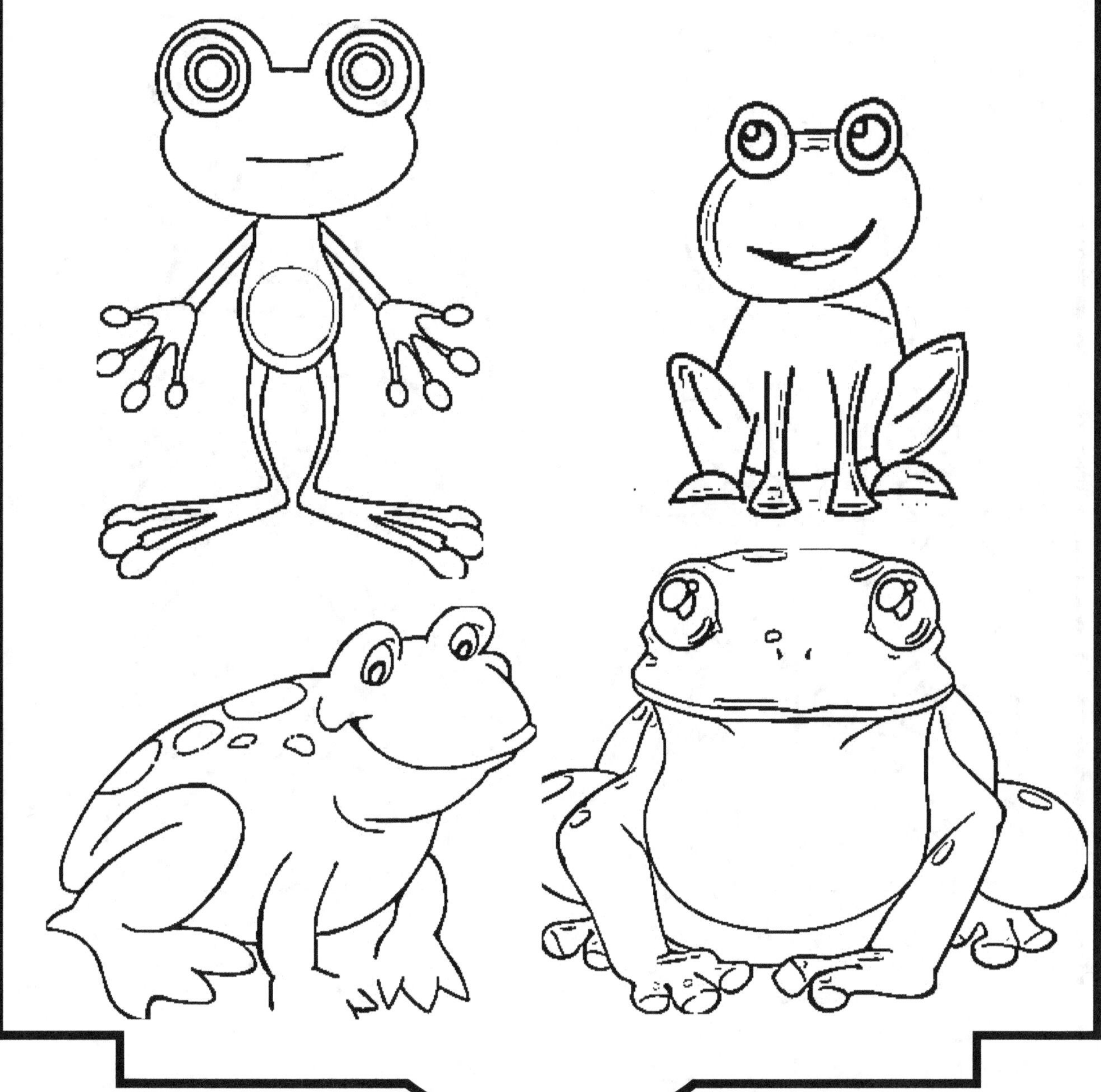

Bear

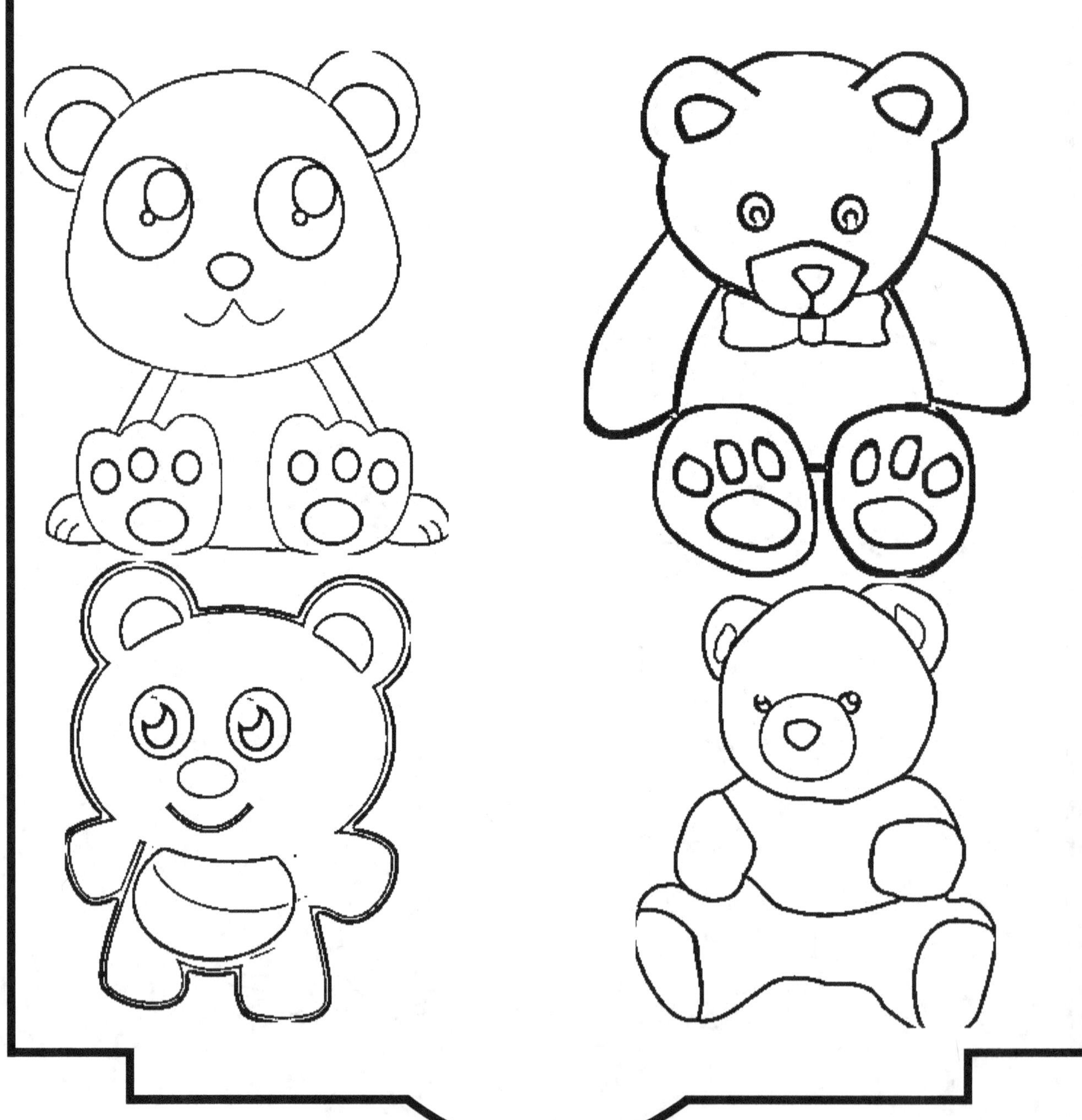

Bee

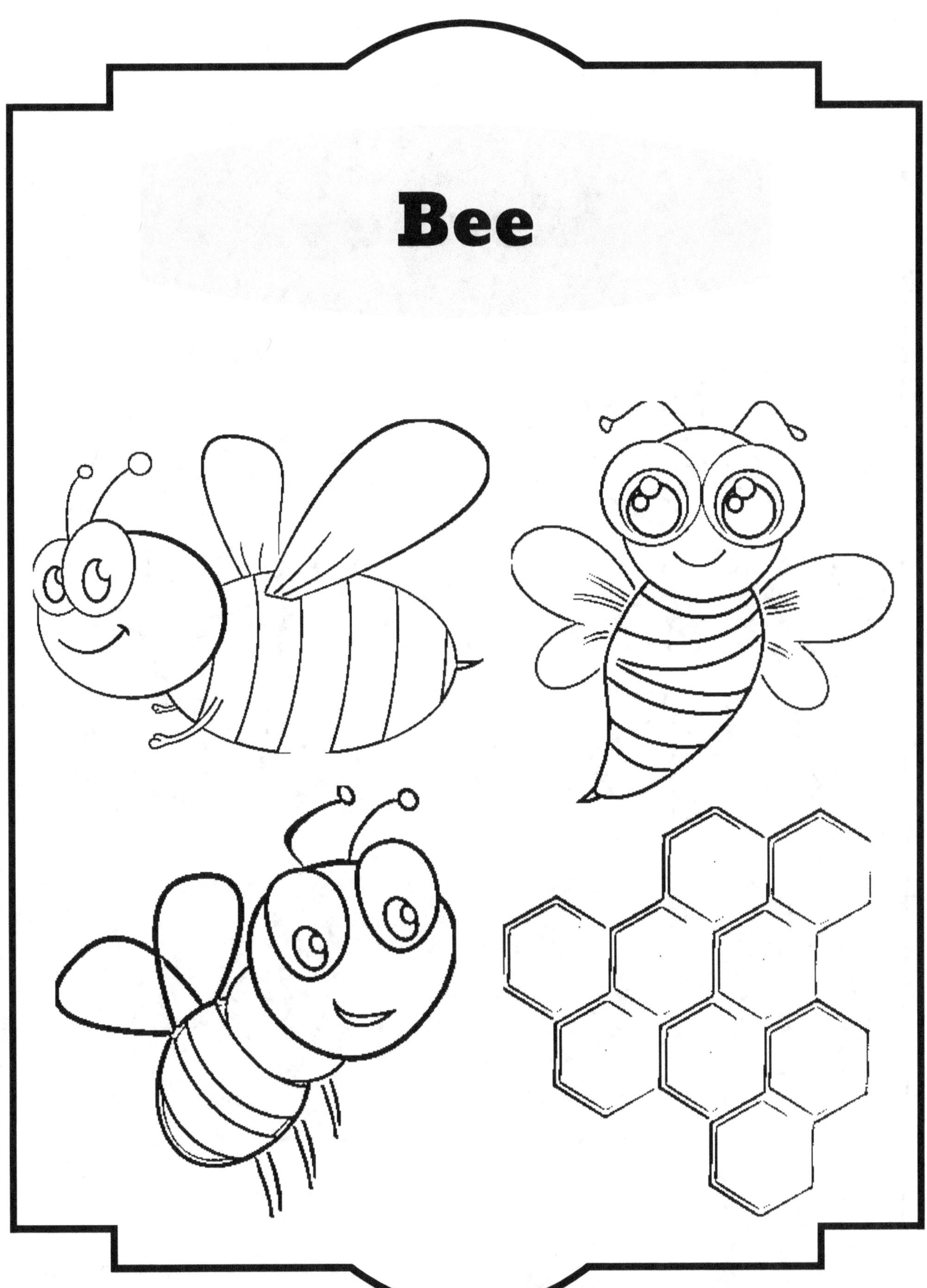

Monkey

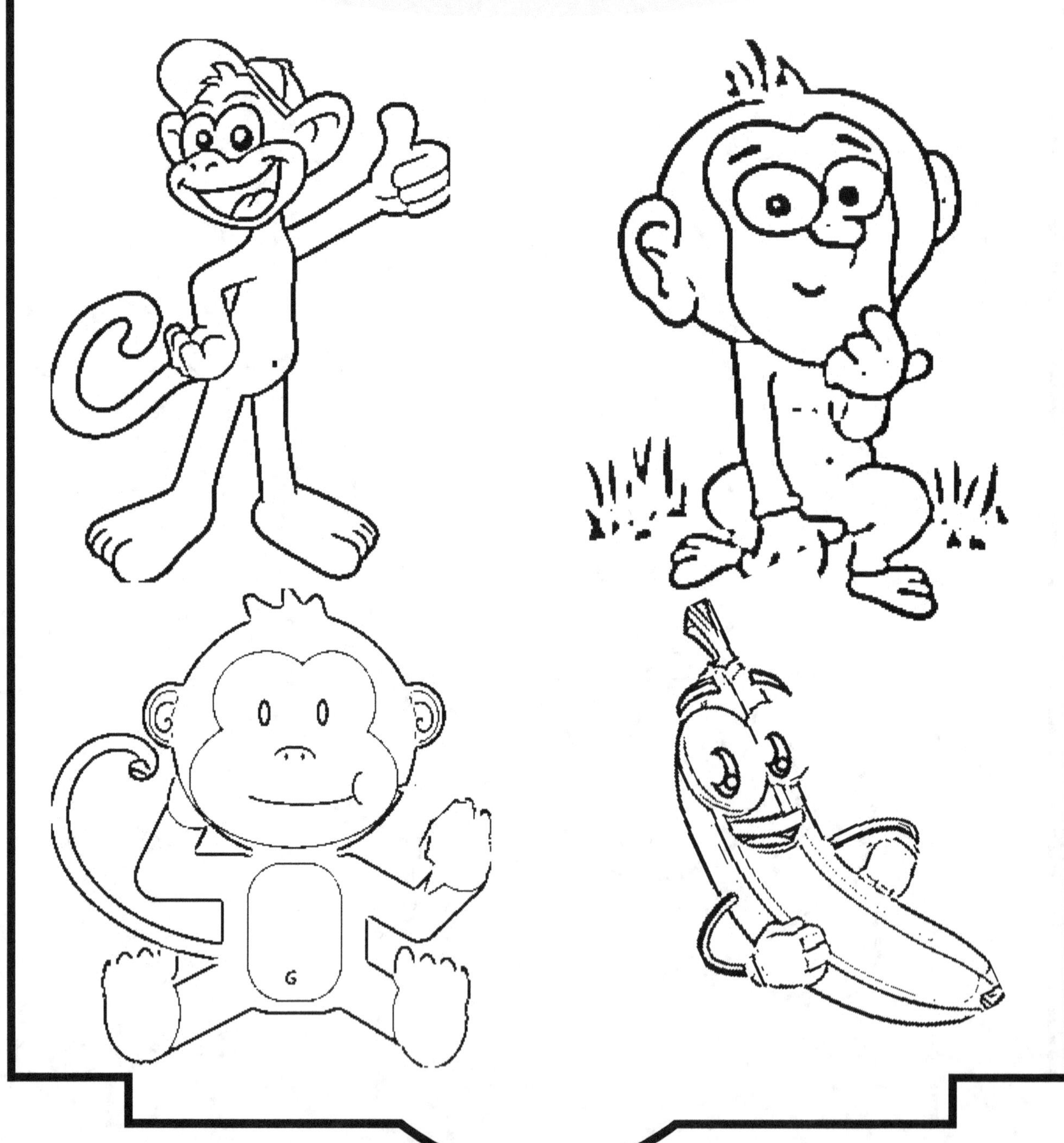

Bird

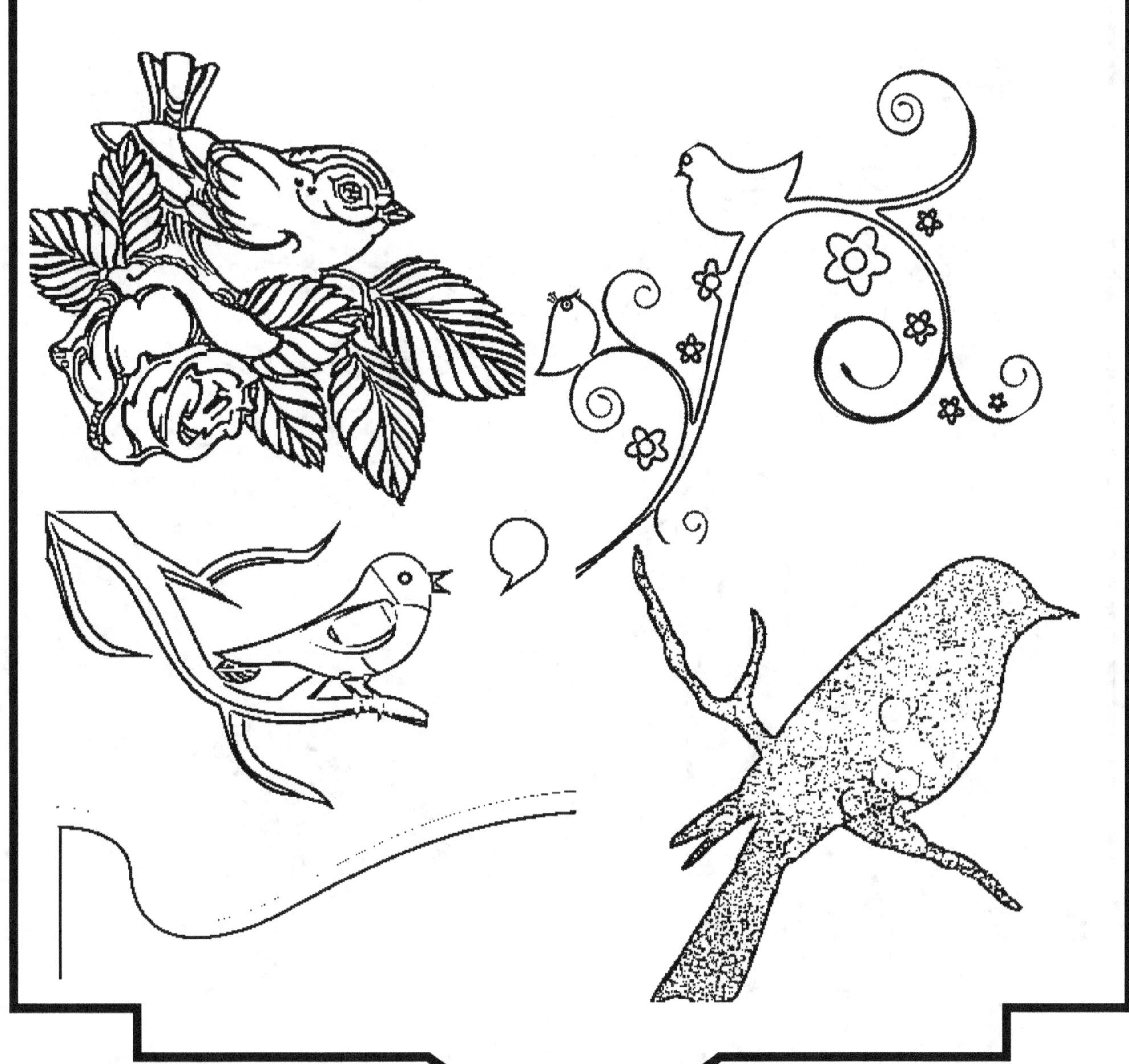

Goose

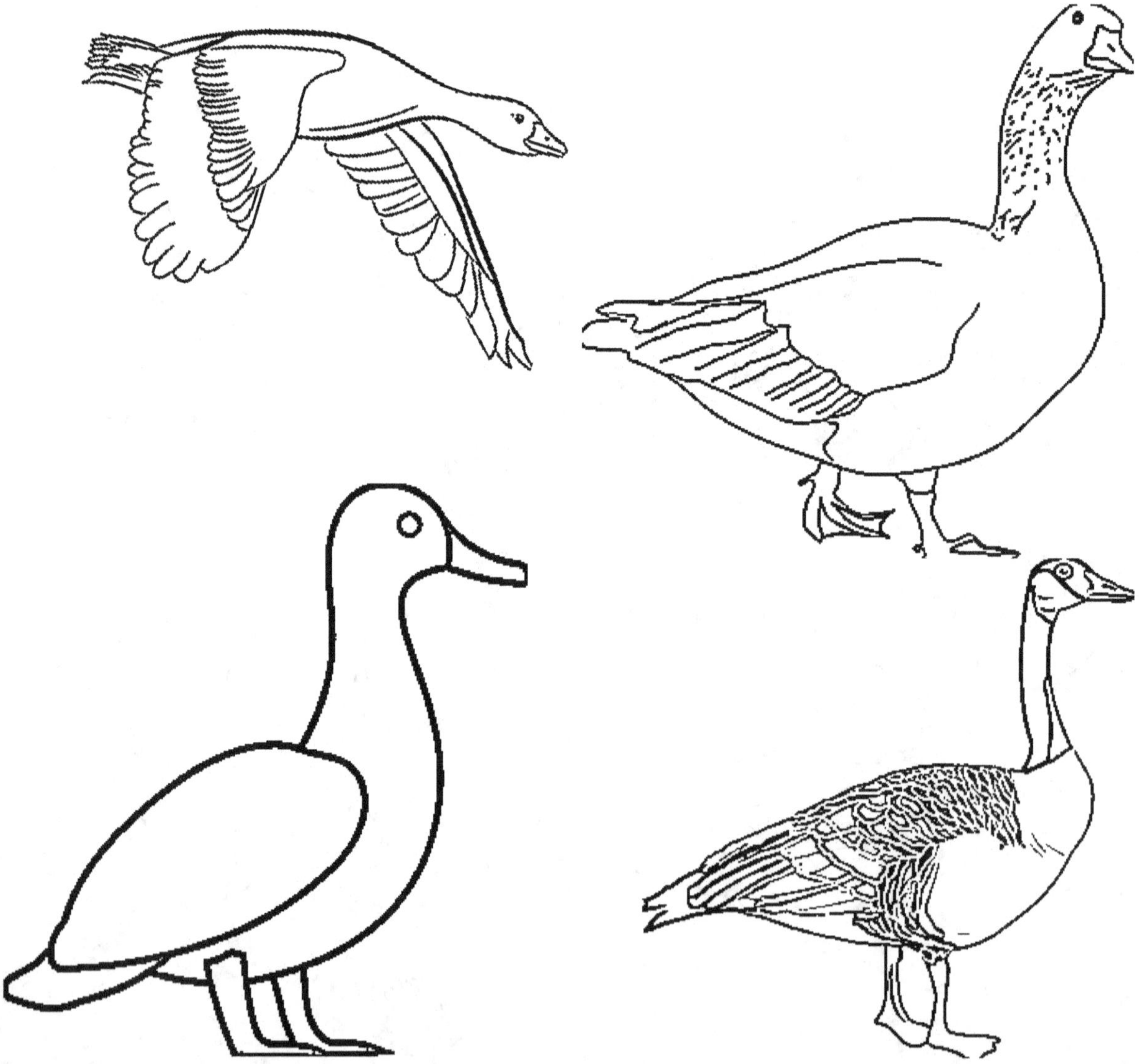

Penguin

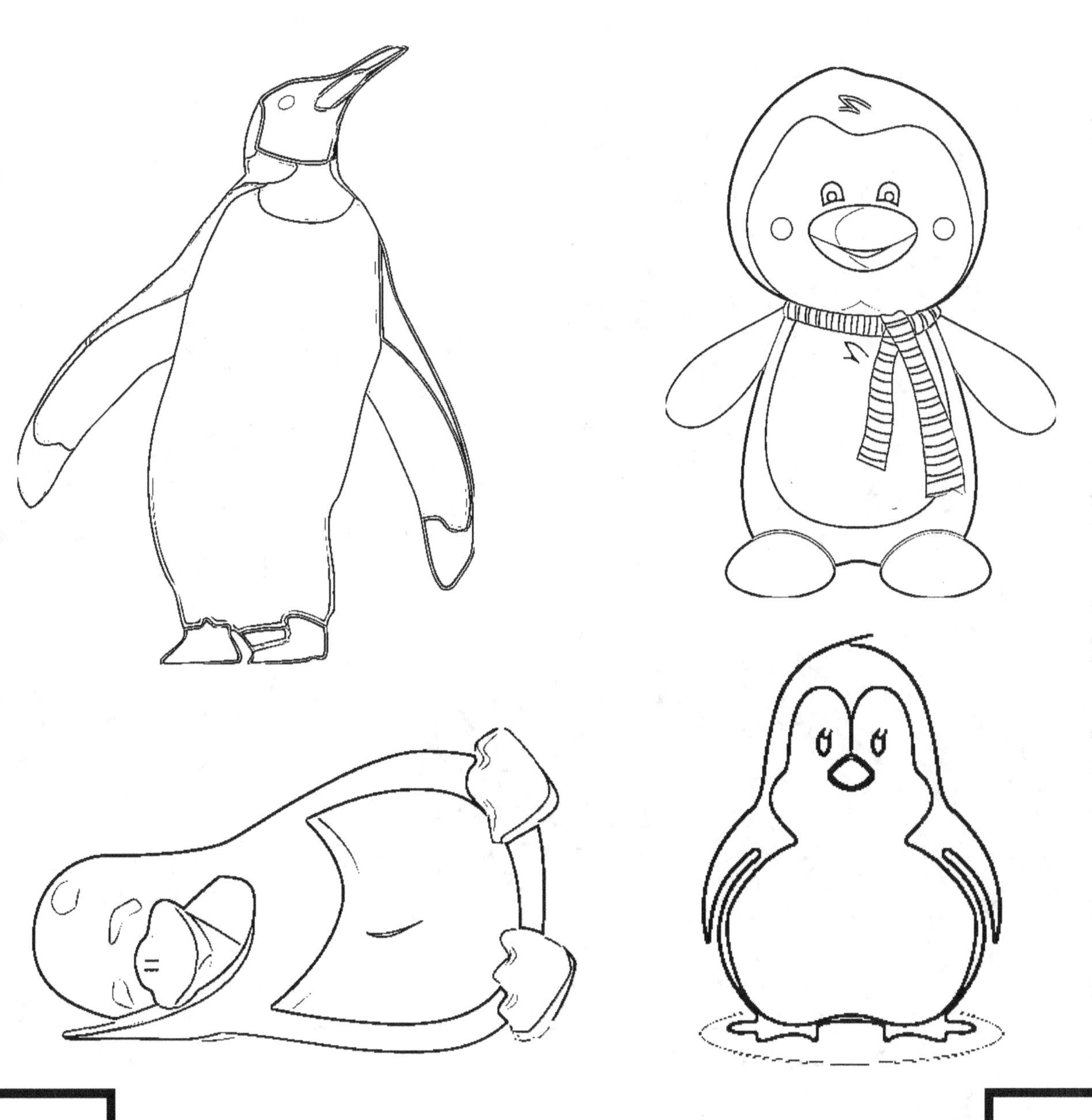

Squirrel

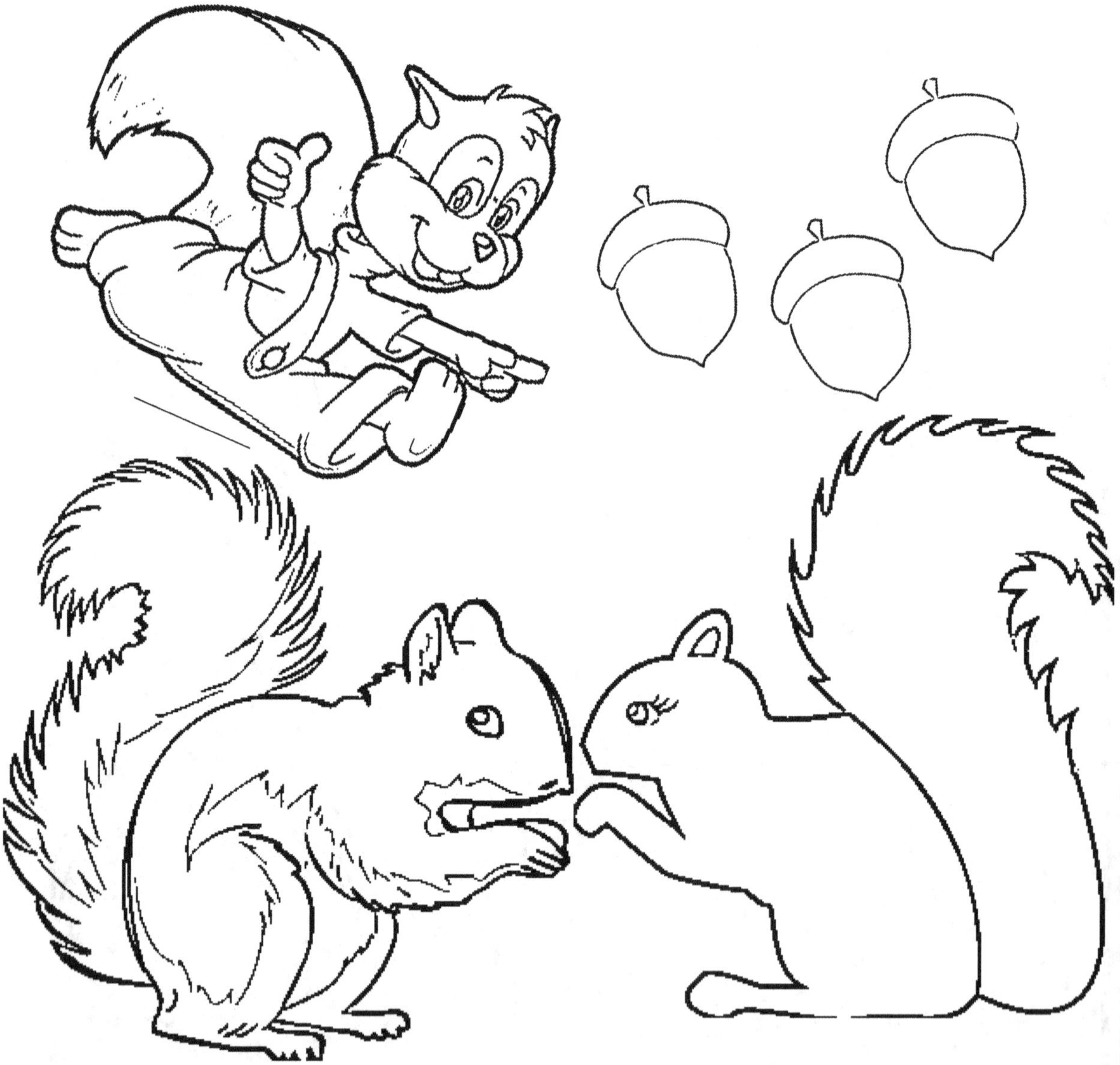